Bradford Railways in Colour
Volume 4: The Midland Lines After Steam

Willowherb Publishing

First published 2022

Willowherb Publishing
www.willowherbpublishing.co.uk

© Alan Whitaker and Jan Rapacz 2022

The right of Alan Whitaker and Jan Rapacz to be identified as the authors of this work has been asserted by them in accordance with the Copyright, Design and Patents Act 1988.

All rights reserved. No part of this book may be reproduced, or utilised in any form, stored or introduced into a retrieval system, or transmitted in any form or by any means (electronic, mechanical, photocopying, recording or otherwise) without prior permission from the Publishers.

Printed in the UK by:
The Amadeus Press
Cleckheaton
BD19 4TQ
ISBN: 978-0-9935678-8-9

Front Cover
31162 arrives at Bradford Valley goods yard on 26 May 1984 with what was, by then, the only train of the day. On this occasion, it is conveying two Ferryvans and an empty wagon which would be dropped off at Crossley's scrap siding at Shipley on the return journey. *(Andrew Rapacz)*

Frontispiece
By the time of this summer 1983 view of Metro-Cammell diesel multiple units at Bradford Forster Square, only three of the station's six platforms were still in regular use. Note the marker tail lamp positioned on Platform 2 to advise the driver of the limit for stopping his train. *(Jan Rapacz Collection)*

Rear Cover
With eight Mk 1 coaches in tow, D200, the first of the English Electric Type 4s, accelerates from Saltaire towards the Hirst Wood foot crossing with the 1605 Leeds to Carlisle on 26 July 1986. The locomotive, which also carried its 40122 TOPS number, was a frequent performer on this service and had 'celebrity' status among enthusiasts. *(Alan Whitaker)*

Introduction

The malaise that hung over Bradford's railways in the years leading up to the end of BR steam in 1968 continued unabated into the 1970s.

After two decades of seemingly relentless closures and service cuts, the city's place on the national network was seriously weakened,

On the south side of the city centre was Exchange station – a decrepit shadow of its former Victorian splendour – while on the north side, was another terminus station at Forster Square which was full of loaded mail order parcels trolleys but not much in the way of passenger train services.

As for the once extensive freight yards which had played a huge role in Bradford's rise to prominence as the 'Wool Capital' of the world, most had gone and the last - Bradford Valley Road - was about to begin a gradual decline which would result in its closure in 1984.

But, in terms of passenger services, things did eventually improve, especially on the former Midland Railway lines out of Forster Square station which are the focus of the book – the fourth and final album in the *Bradford Railways in Colour* series from Willowherb Publishing.

Unlike Exchange station which suffered a slow descent into decrepitude throughout the 1950s/60s, Bradford Forster Square was modernised in 1954. But 19 years on, the roles had been reversed.

In 1973, the old Bradford Exchange was replaced by a new terminus - albeit less than half the size of its predecessor - and became part of a transport Interchange when the adjoining bus station finally opened in 1977 after various delays.

Across the city centre, it was then the turn of Forster Square station to see a downward spiral which would continue until 1990 when it too was replaced by a much smaller new station. And there was more to come.

Electrification of the East Coast Main Line from London King's Cross into Leeds in 1989 triggered an intense campaign by Bradford Council, MPs, the local media and rail users' groups to ensure that the wires did not end there.

The city's 'Electrify Bradford' campaign was a bit of a roller coaster but approval was finally given for the lines from Leeds to Ilkley, Shipley, Bradford Forster Square and Skipton to be electrified and work to build the infrastructure began in 1992.

But then, because of complications associated with the impending privatisation of British Rail, West Yorkshire Passenger Transport Executive was unable to secure funding for new electric trains. This potential embarrassment was overcome when BR offered a fleet of old trains as a stop-gap. It was not an ideal scenario but there was no other option and the vintage units ran for six years until new modern electric trains were finally introduced in 2001.

The upturn in the fortunes of the local rail network can be traced back to 1974 when the West Yorkshire Passenger Transport Executive was formed to take on the responsibility for local public transport strategy and decision-making from BR which had always found closing stations to cut costs easier than trying to develop its existing business.

After years of decline, it was a new dawn but it took quite a while to reverse some of the damage done in the 1960s. The revival on the Airedale and Wharfedale lines out of Bradford Forster Square began slowly in the 1980s when new stations were built to serve Crossflatts, Cononley, Saltaire and Frizinghall. The last three were replacements for what had been lost to a frenzy of BR closures in 1965, while Crossflatts had been waiting for a station to call its own since 1875!

Since then, two more intermediate stations on the Airedale line which closed in 1965 have been restored to the network. These are Steeton & Silsden, opened in 1990, and Apperley Bridge, opened in 2015.

On the Wharfedale line, the ticket offices at Menston and Guiseley stations, which had been unstaffed since 1968, were re-established in 1998 and 2002 respectively, with the latter requiring construction of a new building.

Service improvements and further investment since electrification in 1995 have led to an upturn in patronage which could never have been envisaged half a century ago, but Bradford Forster Square still has the feel of a branch line backwater station.

However, plans for a major modernisation of the 32-year old station have been announced which would improve its nondescript frontage and address its lack of retail, catering and other passenger facilities taken for granted at other big city stations around the country.

Bradford's Achilles Heel as a rail centre has always been its lack of a cross-city 'through' route. Politicians and 'consultants' continue to pontificate about bridging the gap with grandiose schemes but we are no further forward than we were in the late 19th century when the Midland Railway Company drew up plans before getting cold feet and abandoning the idea. Will it ever happen? The cost would be huge so it seems unlikely - but electrification seemed unlikely 50 years ago so who knows what might happen in the next half century.

With 112 pages available, this book can only provide a glimpse into what has happened on Bradford's former Midland lines since 1968 but all the principal changes have been covered. The main focus has been on scenes, locations and motive power types which can no longer be seen rather than operations which are still an everyday sight.

Once again, we are indebted to all the photographers who have willingly and generously allowed us to reproduce their work and also to the contributors who provided information. In particular, we would like to acknowledge the assistance of Martin Bairstow in enabling us to plug gaps in the coverage and enhance the narrative.

Alan Whitaker

August 2022

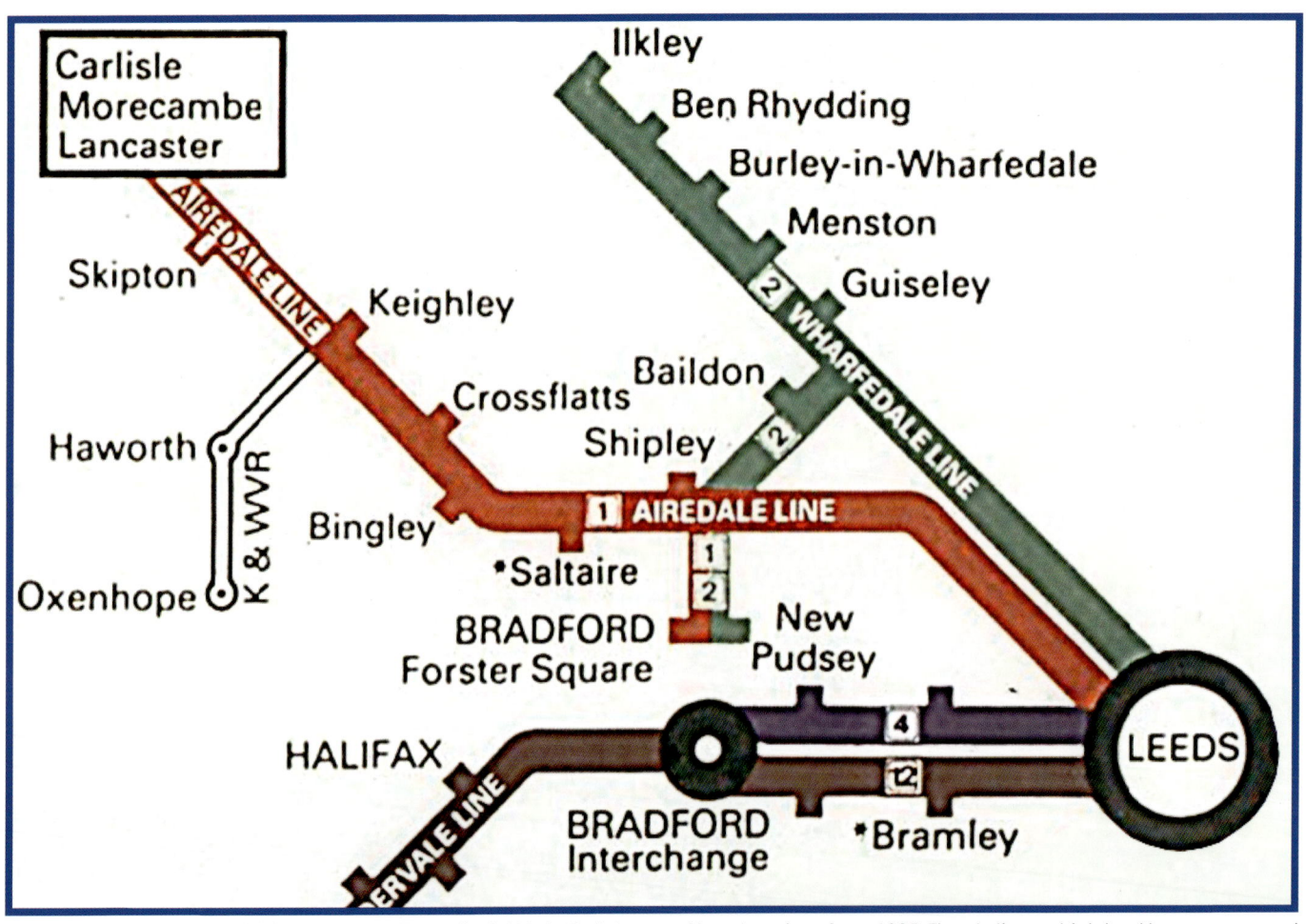

Excerpt from the West Yorkshire Passenger Executive's 'MetroTrain' map of local services from 1985. The stations which had been reopened by that time are shown. There were plenty more to come thanks to the PTE's desire to arrest the years of decline under BR and develop the network. *(West Yorkshire PTE)*

The transfer of long-distance services from Forster Square to Bradford Exchange station in May 1967 made locomotive-hauled trains something of a rarity at the former Midland Railway terminus. However, Leeds Holbeck's Class 24 No. 5097 was unusually rostered for an outing to Morecambe in April 1969 and is seen awaiting departure from Platform 3. The locomotive retains green livery at a time when repainting of main line traction into the new BR corporate blue was accelerating. The first coach also retains its original maroon livery, with the rest of the coaching stock sporting grey and blue colours first trialled in 1964 before being adopted as the new standard a couple of years later. The station canopies and the platform lights both carry the Bradford Forster Square identity and were erected during modernisation of the station in 1954. *(ColourRail)*

More typical of the passenger services in and out of Forster Square station in the late 1960s/early 70s post-steam era were the Airedale and Wharfedale locals to Keighley and Ilkley. Here, the train guard chats with his driver before departure on a BR Derby-built Class 108 DMU to Keighley on 16 May 1970. The unit is showing the B4 two-character headcode for Leeds-Ilkley services rather than the correct code which would have been B1. Running with incorrect codes was not unusual as, by this time, setting the correct display did not seem to feature highly on the list of priorities for some DMU drivers and the practice fell out of use. From 1975 onwards, the headcode equipment was removed and the external screens plated over as part of the DMU fleet refurbishment programme. *(Jan Rapacz Collection)*

Forster Square station on 2 May 1971 was a hive of activity with most lines occupied. In the foreground, a Bradford Hammerton Street-based Class 03 shunts vans in the former Fish Dock sidings which, at this time, served the international freight forwarding firm, Panalpina. Beyond that, a 'Peak' Type 4 diesel awaits departure from Platform 2 with a passenger train diverted from Exchange station due to Sunday engineering work. The School Street bridge runs across the platforms and in front of the Bradford Valley Road goods shed being served by road vehicles in BR's familiar National Carriers yellow livery. *(ColourRail)*

The carriage sidings on the right are full of parcels vans in May 1973 as another 204 horsepower Class 03 diesel shunter reverses away from Forster Square station with the stock of a London to Bradford train diverted from the line into Exchange station because of yet more engineering works. In the distance, a BR Sulzer Type 2 (Class 25) stands at the head of a parcels train in Platform 5 while another train of vans is loaded in the adjacent Platform 4. Business at Valley goods depot also seems to be healthy with plenty of wagons in evidence. *(Roger Hepworth)*

A view looking the other way on the same day finds a three-car Class 110 'Calder Valley' DMU arriving at Forster Square. The B.R.U.T.E. (British Railways Universal Trolley Equipment) trolleys on the platform were a familiar sight during the mail order boom of the 1960s and 70s which provided the station with most of its revenue. Bradford was home to two of the UK's top mail order firms, Grattan and Empire Stores, and almost 1,000 of these trolleys were allocated to Forster Square station to cope with the traffic. Nine parcels trains a day were required for outward traffic from the station in 1973, with 80 per cent of it being mail order business. This amounted to at least 10,000 parcels being handled every weekday, doubling to 20,000 in the run-up to Christmas. Although still quite impressive, this was well down on a few years earlier when 40,000 packages a day were being dealt with by 70 full time staff. In comparison, inward parcels arriving at Forster Square in 1972-73 amounted to about 2,000 a day. *(Roger Hepworth)*

A part of the Bradford landscape which has changed beyond recognition since this 1973 view. The Corporation Electricity Department's Valley Road Power Station dwarfs the scene, with its 300 ft. chimney towering over everything. When it was completed in 1947, the chimney was the tallest in the city. It was demolished in 1978 and the Power Station is also just a memory. The two grounded coach bodies with clerestory roofs in the foreground were used for many years by yard staff. The coach nearest to the camera had been a 3rd Class passenger and baggage car and the other was built as a 1st and 2nd Class composite. Having been designed to resemble American Pullman cars, they were assembled by the Midland Railway Company at Derby in 1874 from parts shipped over from Detroit. After withdrawal, they were grounded for office use. The vintage pair finally left Bradford on 1 May 1975 when they were lifted on to low loaders and taken away for preservation. The 3rd/baggage car is still awaiting restoration at the Midland Railway Centre, Butterley, but the whereabouts of the other is uncertain. (Roger Hepworth)

Although the mail order parcels business at Forster Square station remained reasonably buoyant until the late 1970s, the first signs of rundown are apparent in this view taken on 19 April 1977. A comparison with the photo on Page 8 shows that track has been lifted between the signal box and the huts on the left and the former Midland Railway goods warehouse behind the School Street bridge has gone. This was demolished in 1975 and the site was eventually sold to Royal Mail for redevelopment as the Bradford Mail Centre, part of the panelled stone wall which separated the station's Platform 6 from the side of the goods shed survived the demolition of the old Forster Square station in 1992 and is still standing. It now borders an office block. On the right, a Class 08 diesel shunter rests in the carriage sidings. These 350 horsepower locomotives were supplied by Leeds Holbeck shed, having replaced the smaller Class 03s from Bradford Hammerton Street which had worked Forster Square pilot duties for many years. *(Jan Rapacz Collection)*

The evening Bradford Forster Square to Bolton parcels train sets out behind Sheffield Tinsley's 'Peak' No. 45032 on a sunny 14 June 1979. There were still parcels services to several destinations at this time but it was a last hurrah as things were already changing as more and more mail order traffic was being switched to road transport. The curtain came down in 1980 when BR abandoned its Collection & Delivery parcels service, leaving much of Forster Square station redundant. Freight traffic from Valley goods yard still seems fairly healthy with mineral wagons and Ferryvans filling the sidings. 45032 was new in July 1961 as D38. It received its BR Total Operations Processing System (TOPS) number early in 1975 and continued in service until December 1980. After 2½ years awaiting its fate, the locomotive was scrapped in 1983. *(John S. Whiteley)*

Wind forward 3½ years to early 1983 and two of Forster Square station's six platforms have been taken out of use. Here, a weekend engineering train, with Class 31 No. 31249 in charge, stands in the disused Platform 6 under the School Street bridge. This platform had been shortened from its original length by 10 yards in May 1980. Two more platforms were closed as part of a programme of 'improvement' works in September 1983, leaving only Platforms 1 and 2 operational. The works also included track layout alterations and the installation of colour lights to replace the old semaphore signals. The ornate ironwork featuring a Midland Railway wyvern is well illustrated in this view. Just visible behind the bridge on the left is the end wall of the new Bradford Mail Centre opened by Royal Mail in 1981, six years after demolition of the former Midland Railway goods warehouse which had occupied the site. *(Andrew Rapacz)*

13

The disused West Carriage Sidings at Bradford Forster Square were unexpectedly brought back into use in June 1983 for the storage of withdrawn Class 306 electric multiple units from Essex. The first sets arrived on Wednesday, 29 June and stirred much interest among local railway enthusiasts, many of whom had never seen a Class 306. More of the former Ilford-based units, which had been synonymous with the Great Eastern suburban lines out of London, subsequently arrived and some were stored in the disused part of Forster Square station. This line-up, headed by set 010, is seen in Platform 5 on 2 November 1983. Having been withdrawn in 1981, this set had been stored at Chadwell Heath before being brought to Bradford where it remained until 29 June 1984 – exactly one year to the day after the first Class 306s arrived in the city. It was then dragged to Tinsley yard at Sheffield, along with the others in this view (sets 015 and 080), prior to making its final journey to the West Midlands for scrapping. The sets which had been stored in the old carriage sidings had left a few days earlier. *(Alan Whitaker)*

A two-car Class 101 Metro-Cammell DMU, in grey and blue 'MetroTrain livery, is about to pass the impressive Bradford Forster Square signal box with an off-peak service to Skipton on 19 May 1984. Ten of these units were modified in the early 1960s to incorporate a roof-mounted headcode box which required the destination indicator panel to be placed lower down, thereby reducing the height of the middle window. By the time of this view, the redundant headcode box had been removed leaving the smaller middle window the only clue to this earlier modification. The signal box was nearing the end of its career and was de-commissioned five months later, on 21 October 1984, along with Manningham Junction box. Control of the lines into Forster Square station's two remaining operational platforms and access into Valley goods yard then became the responsibility of the Shipley Bradford Junction duty signalman. Forster Square and Manningham Junction boxes had been made redundant by the completion of extensive track and signalling alterations between Shipley and Bradford. *(Andrew Rapacz)*

The decline of freight traffic in and out of Bradford Valley through the 1970s was in stark contrast to what was happening in the immediate post-steam period of the late 60s. Closure of Manningham steam locomotive shed in April 1967 saw the remaining local goods services in Airedale and Wharfedale – and on the former GNR branch between Shipley and Idle – converted to diesel haulage. Many longer distance freights had been diesel-hauled well before the end of the steam era, with Sulzer Type 2 (Class 25) and 'Peak' Type 4s of Classes 45 and 46 the usual motive power. Here, a Leeds Holbeck-based Class 25, No. D5254, in its original two-tone green livery, waits to ease a lengthy mixed freight out of the Trafalgar sidings. Another mixed rake in an adjoining siding is being checked by a member of the depot's staff who is walking alongside with his shunting pole. The Trafalgar Street freight forwarding sheds can be seen to good effect on the right. Trafalgar had been a separate depot until 1962 when it became part of the Valley Road operation. *(D.J. Mitchell)*

English Electric Type 4s (Class 40) became increasingly regular visitors to Bradford Valley yard from the mid-1970s. On this occasion, 40007 stands in the sun at the top end of the yard, having been coupled to a train of vans. This locomotive, which entered service in July 1958 as D207, was one of the pioneers of the changeover from steam to diesels on East Anglian express services between Norwich, Harwich and London Liverpool Street. At the time of this view, it was based at Healey Mills, near Wakefield, and continued in service until February 1983 when it was withdrawn as a result of derailment damage sustained at Llandudno. *(Gavin Morrison)*

The Brush Type 2 (Class 31) was another diesel loco type which became familiar on freight services in and out of Bradford Valley from the mid-1970s when the more established Class 25s were ousted from many of their former duties. A lull in shunting operations on 23 April 1980 finds snowplough-fitted 31111 under the iron footbridge which spanned Valley goods yard and linked Midland Road with Snowden Street. The locomotive started life as D5529 at March shed (Cambridgeshire) in May 1959 and was one of the early batches of Brush Type 2s fitted with front discs rather than roof-mounted headcode boxes. At the time of this photo, it was based at York but was already a familiar sight in the area having been allocated to Leeds Holbeck for several years from 1974. 31111 was prematurely withdrawn after its engine exploded while working near Peterborough in 1983. Having donated one of its cabs to classmate 31444, it was then scrapped. *(John S. Whiteley)*

Another of the pioneering late 1950s Great Eastern main line Class 40s, No. 40006 (formerly D206), waits to be detached from its train of mineral wagons alongside the National Carriers Trafalgar Street freight forwarding shed in 1982. Bradford Trafalgar goods depot had been amalgamated into the Valley Road operation 20 years earlier, on 22 October 1962, as part of a scheme to streamline rail freight facilities in the city centre. This was prompted by the closure of the former Lancashire & Yorkshire Railway's Bridge Street depot which took effect on the same date and included the transfer of some staff to Valley. Judging by what can be seen through the open door, the Trafalgar warehouse, which was partly reconstructed in 1973 to increase freight handling capacity, was still doing good business but it wouldn't last much longer. *(Jan Rapacz)*

The use of Leeds Holbeck-based Class 08 shunters as pilot locomotives for the Bradford Forster Square parcels traffic and the Valley goods yard duties was relatively short-lived. These locos had begun to appear in 1972, initially sharing duties with smaller Class 03s from Bradford Hammerton Street which were later phased out. However, closure of Holbeck as a maintenance depot in 1978 resulted in many of its shunters being transferred to Hammerton Street which once again took on responsibility for supplying the Forster Square and Valley pilots. The lack of a 'through' route in Bradford meant a long detour via Leeds to enable the locos to reach the other side of the city centre. On duty in Valley yard on this occasion in 1982 was 08369 which was one of the shunters transferred from Leeds to Bradford in October 1978. This transfer represented a return 'home' for the locomotive which, as D3454, had been new to Hammerton Street shed in May 1957. Shunting locomotives were no longer required at Bradford Valley after the depot was reduced to an unstaffed Public Delivery Siding not long after this photo was taken. *(Jan Rapacz)*

It is 26 May 1984 and, with only six more weeks to go before closure, Bradford Valley yard is host to 31162 which has arrived with the morning freight, comprising two Continental Ferryvans and an empty wagon destined for Crossley's siding at Shipley where it would be filled with scrap metal for onward transit to Sheerness in Kent. This loco had entered service at Norwich in January 1960 as D5580 and was renumbered into the TOPS system in 1973. It was based at Healey Mills when seen here but was transferred to Bescot (Birmingham) a few weeks later. It was withdrawn in 1992. The covered loading dock with the blue canopy at the south side of Forster Square station on the right, was the 'Fish Dock' where consignments of fish, meat and other fresh produce were unloaded for many years. The dock was latterly used by international freight forwarding and logistics company Panalpina but had fallen into disuse by the time of this view. The Fish Dock was reached by an inclined approach from Cheapside which now provides a pedestrian access to the 'new' Forster Square station, opened in 1990. *(Andrew Rapacz)*

BRADFORD VALLEY
Public Delivery Siding

The Eastern Region of British Rail announce that the above depot will be closed on and from **Monday, August 6th 1984.**

Alternative facilities for traffic in full wagon loads, other than **Coal Class Traffic** will be available at **Leeds, Whitehall Road** or **Dewsbury, Railway Street.**

Coal Class Traffic may be dealt with under special arrangements only.

Further information may be obtained from The Area Manager, Leeds
Telephone: Leeds 431711

F. Paterson
General Manager
British Rail Eastern Region
York.

After the progressive abandonment of many of its sidings from 1969 onwards, the downgrading of the once extensive Valley goods depot to an unstaffed Public Delivery Siding left it vulnerable and, in January 1984, BR announced that it would close in May. This was subsequently put back and a revised official closure date of Monday 6 August 1984 was later confirmed. A notice to that effect was stuck in the window of one of the offices near the yard entrance and stated that alternative facilities for full wagonload traffic would be available at Leeds Whitehall Road and at Dewsbury Railway Street – both convenient for Bradford customers, of course. The notice also pointed out that coal class traffic 'may be dealt with under special arrangements only.' In other words, we'd rather not bother. *(Alan Whitaker)*

Immingham's 31288 had the honour of working the last loaded freight train into Bradford Valley yard on Friday 3 August 1984. It arrived 20 minutes late at 0740 with one single Ferryvan in tow. The locomotive then collected three loaded Ferryvans and an empty wagon to be dropped off at Crossley's siding at Shipley and departed just after 8 o'clock. The single Ferryvan which had been left would be collected the following week after it had been loaded, even though the yard was officially closed. The 'Last Freight – Valley Road' commemorative headboard adorning the front of the locomotive was made by local photographer Andrew Rapacz who can be seen to the left of the loco. Some of his work is featured in this book, including the front cover image. Having secured its place in Bradford railway history, 31288 continued in service until 1991, thirty years after its introduction as D5820. It was scrapped in 1992. *(Alan Whitaker)*

Engineering work on the line into Bradford Exchange on Sunday 16 September 1979 saw Inter-City services diverted to Forster Square. Here, an empty High Speed Train in original livery passes Manningham Junction on its way into the station where it would form the 0831 service to London King's Cross. The leading power car is 43076 which would be the rear car on departure from Forster Square. The power car at the other end was 43087 which is just out of view. The lines into Bradford Valley goods yard can be seen on the right. One of these was removed in 1980 when single line operation into and out of the yard was implemented. *(John S. Whiteley)*

A mixed freight for Healey Mills sets out from Bradford Valley behind Sulzer Class 25 No. 25145 on 22 April 1982. At the front are two VTG Ferrywagon bogie vans carrying Continental traffic from international freight forwarders Panalpina. These would be staged at Healey Mills pending onward transit. The three empty mineral wagons before the brake van at the rear are evidence that coal traffic was still being handled at Valley but it was dwindling. The locomotive's home base at this time was Cricklewood (London) so it was a rare visitor to Bradford. *(John S. Whiteley)*

The day after the photograph on the previous page, 40198 trundles past Manningham Junction signal box on an engineers' train bound for Bradford Valley. Comparison with the view on Page 24 shows the modified track layout with one line now truncated at a buffer stop and the line nearest to the boundary wall separating the railway from Valley Road having been lifted. Manningham Junction signal box closed on 21 October 1984 – the same day as the Forster Square station box. All movements in and out of the station were then controlled from Shipley Bradford Junction box. 40198 was new as D398 in 1962 and was a Healey Mills loco for most of its life. It was withdrawn in January 1983 - eight months after this photograph was taken. *(John S. Whiteley)*

Periodic diversions into Forster Square station when engineering works blocked the line between Leeds and Bradford Exchange during the 1970s usually grabbed the attention of local photographers. Here, a Class 47 approaches its destination with a Sunday service from London King's Cross in May 1973. The train has just passed the site of Manningham station, closed in 1965. The wasteland on the right was once occupied by the Manningham steam locomotive depot which closed in April 1967 and stood empty until its demolition in the autumn of 1968. This view shows how the passenger lines had been slewed on to what had been the goods lines so they could by-pass the Manningham station site. This work had taken place in 1970. The Siphon van off its bogies on the left is awaiting disposal having had a bit of a whack. *(Roger Hepworth)*

Frizinghall was one of ten intermediate stations between Bradford Forster Square, Leeds and Skipton which closed in March 1965. BR had also wanted to close the entire line between Shipley, Guiseley and Ilkley but the Secretary of State deferred the decision following strong public opposition which focused attention on the route and led to increased use of the services. However, Wharfedale did not emerge unscathed as closures of the lines between Ilkley and Skipton via Bolton Abbey and from Menston Junction to Otley and Arthington were approved. Here, a Class 101 DMU, with car 50154 leading, passes the site of Frizinghall station with the 1430 from Ilkley to Bradford Forster Square on a dull 13 April 1974. The remnants of the former goods lines can be seen on the right. These were closed in May 1970 but a short section of one of them was retained from Manningham Junction to provide access to a delivery siding. This connection was abolished in March 1972. *(Clive Weston)*

The 1965 closures ended up costing the next generation of taxpayers a fortune as replacement stations have since been built at many of the locations which lost their passenger services on the back of the short-sighted decisions of the time. In terms of facilities, the new stations are all fairly basic but they are better than nothing. Only 15 years after Frizinghall's 1875 stone-built station was bulldozed, a new halt with wooden platforms was opened on 7 September 1987. Unlike its predecessor which had facing platforms, the new station was built with platforms staggered on either side of the Frizinghall Road bridge. This view of 'Pacer' unit 144007 on an off-peak service from Guiseley to Bradford Forster Square dates from 12 September 1987 - five days after opening. Construction work in the entrance area was still awaiting completion because the opening had been rushed to coincide with start of the new term at nearby Bradford Grammar School. It quickly became clear that the number of pupils gathering at the same time to catch their trains home was too great for the Ilkley/ Skipton platform to safely cope with and it had to be widened. *(Martin Bairstow)*

A Birmingham Railway Carriage and Wagon Company Class 104 DMU, led by power car No. 50596, passes Shipley Town goods yard on a Bradford Forster Square to Ilkley service on 9 April 1974. By this time, BR operations at the depot had ceased and the site was occupied by local scrap metal recyclers Crossley Brothers who sent out regular trainloads of scrap to various destinations. This justified retention of the sidings and some modest spending by BR on new fences and gates in 1971/72. Note the old Midland Railway hut on the left, boarded up but still standing amid the scrap. The former Shipley (Midland) goods warehouse in the middle distance had fallen into disuse but its access siding was still in place. Shipley was once served by two railway goods depots – the other being the former Great Northern Railway's facility at Windhill which closed in October 1968. The ex-Midland yard was renamed Shipley Town by BR in 1951 to reflect its more central location and to distinguish it from the ex-GN yard. *(Stuart Baker)*

The 1650 Sunday service from Bradford to Birmingham, diverted to start at Forster Square because of engineering works on the line into Exchange station, is seen passing Crossley's sidings at Shipley on 16 September 1979. The firm, which was soon to become Crossley Evans Ltd., was still using 16T mineral wagons for its traffic but these were later replaced by bigger bulk carriers, as seen at Bradford Valley on Page 21. The locomotive in charge is 'Peak' No. 45031, which was allocated to Sheffield Tinsley at the time. It entered service in 1961 as D36 and was among the last in its class to receive its Class 45 TOPS number – this being applied in May 1975. It was withdrawn in May 1981 and scrapped at Derby Works a few months later. *(John S. Whiteley)*

An 'over the wall' view of Class 31 No. 31145 shunting the Crossley Evans sidings before departure with a train of scrap bound for Sheerness on 12 September 1988. This locomotive was new in 1959 and still had plenty of life left in it, surviving in service until the end of the century before being scrapped. It is sporting BR 'large logo' grey livery with full yellow cab ends which was introduced for freight locomotives from late 1982 before Railfreight operations were split into separate sectors, each with their own branding. Class 31s were replaced on these trains by Class 37s in 1990 and Class 56s then took over as the regular motive power in 1993. In the background are two diminutive four-wheeled Ruston & Hornby diesel shunters which were owned by the Crossley Evans company but stored out of use for years. *(Alan Whitaker)*

A two-car Class 101 Metro-Cammell DMU slows into Shipley's Platform 4 with an off-peak Ilkley to Bradford Forster Square service on 12 May 1972. The unit is showing a 2B headcode which is meaningless. It should have been set as B6 but, by this time, correct exposures on local DMUs were becoming rare. Some of the station's 1950s enamel signage is still in place and the iron canopy columns look as though they would benefit from a lick of paint. The surface of the opposite platform is clearly uneven in parts and, overall, the scene exudes an air of decline from a bygone age. All that would change in the 1990s. The gantries in the distance show that Shipley was still signalled for four tracks to Thackley Junction in 1972 but the junction signal arm for the former Great Northern branch to Laisterdyke had been removed from the end of Platform 3 in June 1969. The last operational section of this branch had been abandoned nine months earlier with the closure of Idle goods yard in October 1968. *(Stuart Baker)*

Platforms 1 and 2 at Shipley station were on a tight curve and, after the introduction of longer coaching stock mounted on bogies, trains could not be signalled in both directions between the Bingley and Bradford Junctions. This meant that only one train at a time could pass through or occupy either of the platforms and timetables were set accordingly. A Keighley to Bradford Forster Square local, formed of a BR Class 108 DMU twin set, is seen awaiting departure from Platform 2 on 29 March 1974. The leading car is No. 50602 which is incorrectly showing the B6 headcode for the Ilkley line. Platform 1, on which the photographer is standing, was abandoned in March 1980 when the line between Bingley and Bradford Junctions was singled through Platform 2. However, the Midland Railway wrought iron and glass canopy survived until December 1992 when it was demolished. Platform 2 had already lost its canopy by the time of this view. *(Martin Bairstow)*

A mixed rake of empty stock - including a Mk. 1 buffet car - is about to pass Shipley Bradford Junction behind Leeds Holbeck's Class 31 No. 31410 on 20 April 1975. This unusual movement is believed to have been related to weekend diversions when Bradford Forster Square station was used for InterCity services instead of Bradford Exchange. 31410 was one of 70 in its class fitted with electric train heating equipment for working regional semi-fast passenger trains. This group of locos was re-designated Class 31/4 and continued to perform these duties until being displaced by 'Super Sprinter' DMUs in the late 1980s/early 90s. The faded appearance of 31410 suggests that it would not be too long before it was called in for a new paint job. The locomotive was new as D5669 in November 1960 and lasted in service for 42½ years. It was withdrawn in June 2003 and scrapped the following year. *(Willowherb Publishing Archive)*

The daily London St. Pancras to Glasgow Central (formerly the *Thames-Clyde Express*) was forced to deviate to the wrong side of the Shipley triangle on 31 August 1975 when the main line avoiding curve was blocked by an engineering possession. Instead, the train had to pass through Shipley station's Platform 4 before coming to a stop beyond Shipley Bradford Junction where it had to wait for another locomotive to be attached. The stock, which had been brought from Leeds by a Class 40, can be seen in the distance as 'Peak' No. 45047 negotiates the junction on its way to couple up. The Leeds Holbeck-based 'Peak' had been sent to Shipley earlier to await the arrival the Glasgow train which it would take forward. The *Thames-Clyde Express* title, which dated back to 1927, was ditched by BR from the start of the May 1974 timetable. *(Willowherb Publishing Archive)*

With a Class 31 in attendance, the engineering works blocking the Shipley Curve on 31 August 1975 are seen to good effect in this view as 45047 slowly draws the Glasgow train through the Bradford to Keighley platform to regain its route at Bingley Junction. Full length loco-hauled passenger trains on this part of the Shipley triangle had been virtually unknown since 1967 so this was a photo opportunity not to be missed. The line diverging behind the signal box was the connection to the 'Angle Sidings' which were originally used for unloading wagons of coal for Shipley Gasworks. Latterly, they were used for stabling permanent way wagons, as seen here. The connection to the sidings was severed in September 1978 and the site now forms part of the station car park. 45047 was new in 1960 as D69 and spent its first 12 years allocated to BR's Midland Lines and Nottingham Divisions. It was transferred to Holbeck in 1972 and stayed for five years before moving to Sheffield Tinsley from where it ended its days in 1980. It was broken up at Derby Works in 1981. *(Willowherb Publishing Archive)*

The driver of Class 40 No. 40036 eases up a notch with a lengthy ballast train from Ribblehead quarry to Healey Mills as it comes off the Shipley Curve and on to the Leeds Road bridge on a rather overcast 18 April 1975. These trains were a regular feature of Aire Valley freight traffic for many years, with Class 40s the favoured motive power until the early 1980s when other types started to appear. 40036 was part of the Healey Mills diesel depot allocation in April 1975 so it was on its way home. It was transferred to Wigan Spring's Branch in February 1976, after which it became a nomad, working from Carlisle, Gateshead, Healey Mills again, Thornaby-on-Tees and finally back for a third stint at Healey Mills from where it was withdrawn in January 1982. It was then sent to the 'diesel graveyard' at Swindon Works where it was cut up a few months later. *(Willowherb Publishing Archive)*

This view will be familiar to anyone who witnessed freight traffic on the Airedale line in the 1970s. The 'Tilcon' limestone trains, with their distinctive hopper wagons, were an everyday sight – even running at weekends and, sometimes, during the night. The trains served the Swinden Quarry, near Rylstone, between Skipton and Grassington, which was the last branch line on BR to be operated by steam. Diesels took over when steam bowed out in August 1968 and the traffic has continued to flourish. Today, bulk trains of limestone weighing up to 2,800 tons are hauled by GBRf Class 66/7s which leave the quarry every weekday for Hunslet (Leeds) or Hull, from where the material is exported. But going back to 1970s, pairs of Class 25s were still the mainstay of these services, supplemented by Class 40s if required. Here 25204 leads classmate 25199 past Shipley Gasworks with the Tilcon empties from Hull to Swinden Quarry on 17 June 1975. The leading loco came to a premature end when it was withdrawn as a result of collision damage in 1980, aged just 15. Its partner lasted seven years longer, being withdrawn in 1987. *(Willowherb Publishing Archive)*

A lengthy mixed freight from Carlisle New Yard to Healey Mills approaches Guiseley Junction behind Class 40 No. 40198 on 3 May 1982. These heavy trains had been long established on the Aire Valley main line but times were changing and scenes like this were on borrowed time. The number of tracks between Guiseley Junction and Shipley had been reduced from four to two during 1975 when the remaining pair were slewed over the wide formation to give a better alignment, thereby allowing higher speeds over the junctions. The field to the left is the site of the Great Northern Railway's Shipley (Windhill) goods yard which closed in 1968. 40198 was no stranger to the area. Apart from a brief period allocated to York in 1969, the locomotive had been Healey Mills-based since 1966 and was seen quite frequently on Bradford Valley and long distance freight workings through Airedale. But its time was drawing to a close and it was withdrawn in January 1983. Having donated useable spares to keep some of its classmates going, it was scrapped. (John S. Whiteley)

A regular performer on the Airedale line in the mid-1980s was 40122 which frequently worked the 1040 Carlisle-Leeds and afternoon return. This was a true celebrity loco. As one of the pioneers of main line dieselisation, it was a significant machine, both culturally and historically. Numbered D200, it was the first of 200 English Electric Type 4s to enter service between 1958-62. It became somewhat anonymous when it took its 40122 TOPS identity which would have been allocated to D322 had it not been wrecked in a collision with runaway freight wagons in May 1966. By the early 1980s, 40122 was in urgent need of repairs but Class 40s were on BR's hit list and the maintenance budget was tight. But because of its significance - which would justify its future place in the National Collection - it was refurbished using donor parts from withdrawn classmates, then repainted in Brunswick green. It also carried both its original number and its TOPS identity. The locomotive attracted a cult following of Class 40 haulage 'bashers' who savoured the experience by hanging out of the carriage windows, as witnessed here as 40122 passes Guiseley Junction signal box with the 1040 from Carlisle on 6 August 1983. (John S. Whiteley)

Pairs of Class 31s became the regular motive power for the Tilcon aggregates trains in the early 1980s and held sway for almost ten years until they were ousted by Class 37s. With a fine view of the Shipley townscape behind, the 1018 from Swinden Quarry to Hull is seen here having just passed Guiseley Junction signal box on 14 June 1983. It is headed by 31163 and 31220 which both entered service in 1960 as D5581 and D5645 respectively. Fate was kinder to the leading loco than to its partner. After withdrawal from service in 1999, 31163 avoided the scrapyard and entered the Departmental loco pool at the Derby Railway Technical Centre which gave it a stay of execution. At the end of its RTC career, it was sold into preservation. 31220 was not so lucky. Having been fitted with electric train heating in 1984, it was renumbered 31441 and could often be seen on the Airedale line working Leeds to Carlisle and Hull to Lancaster trains. The e.t.h. equipment was later removed and it was withdrawn in 1996. After a long period in store, it was scrapped. *(John S. Whiteley)*

42

A local ballast trip working being operated in connection with Sunday engineering works is held at signals at Guiseley Junction on 29 June 1975. The line the train is occupying would be secured out of use within weeks of this view and subsequently lifted. The double track branch to Ilkley (bottom left) was reduced to a single line between Guiseley Junction and Guiseley station in March 1983 which required remodelling of the junction and the installation of new signalling. The leading locomotive is Leeds Holbeck's 31312 (new as D5846 in 1962) which has been paired with York's 31123 (built in 1959 as D5541). Both these locos enjoyed long careers with 31312 lasting in service until 1996 and its older classmate surviving until 1992. *(Willowherb Publishing Archive)*

Exactly a week after the photo on the previous page, more Sunday engineering work at Shipley led to the London St. Pancras to Glasgow Central express having to run wrong line past Thackley Junction signal box. In charge is 'Peak' 45030 (D31 in old money) which was a stalwart on Leeds to Glasgow trains through the Aire Valley for almost 20 years. It was one of a batch of Leeds-based 'Peaks' in the D11-D35 range which became synonymous with express passenger services over the Settle and Carlisle line after taking over from steam in 1961/62. 45030 remained a Leeds loco until the end of 1977 when it was transferred to Sheffield Tinsley but it continued to appear in Airedale until its withdrawal in November 1980. Thackley Junction signal box remained operational until January 1984 when it was abolished following more track and signalling alterations centred on neighbouring Guiseley Junction. *(Willowherb Publishing Archive)*

Although the weather was murky and not ideal for colour photography, the two Thackley Tunnel portals can just be seen in the distance as a Class 108 DMU approaches Apperley Bridge with a Skipton to Leeds train in February 1974. To increase line capacity for heavy freight, the Leeds to Shipley line was widened to four tracks at the turn of the 19th century. This meant that a second Thackley Tunnel had to be constructed alongside the original 1846 bore, which is the one to the left. This tunnel was abandoned in 1968 when the four track section was reduced to two. The lines were then lifted, as can be seen here. The 'new' tunnel from which the DMU had just emerged opened in 1901 and is now the only route under the hill. The siding diverging to the right connected with the Esholt Sewage Works Railway, opened in 1910 by Bradford Corporation to deal with sewage and trade effluent from its many factories and woollen mills. Coal for the works was left in an exchange siding adjacent to the main line and then collected by an ESWR locomotive. At its peak, the standard gauge system had 22 miles of track and 11 locomotives. It closed in 1977. *(Geoff Brown)*

The Esholt Sewage Works Railway's exchange siding connections provide the vantage point for this view of 'Peak' No. 190 as at accelerates towards Thackley Tunnel with 1S49, the 1035 Leeds to Glasgow Central, in the early Spring of 1969. This locomotive was among the last of its class to be built, entering service at Gateshead in January 1963. It was one of 56 Class 46 'Peaks' distinguished from their more numerous Class 45 counterparts simply by having a Brush generator and traction motors rather than the standard Crompton Parkinson equipment fitted to the others. 190 was one of several Gateshead Class 46s transferred to supplement Leeds Holbeck's fleet after the depot's closure to steam in September 1967. It stayed until July 1970 then returned to Gateshead. This loco will be seen again later in the book, carrying its TOPS number 46053 which it received in 1974. The roof of Apperley Viaduct signal box can be seen above the train. Among its duties, this box controlled access to the Sewage Works siding. It was abolished in 1976. *(Willowherb Publishing Archive)*

The scars of track-lifting and the demolition of Apperley Bridge station in the late 1960s are still starkly evident in this May 1976 view of a four-car BRCW Class 104 DMU heading through on the 1712 Leeds to Morecambe service. The station had closed in March 1965 as part of the cull of intermediate stations between Leeds, Bradford Forster Square and Skipton. Although the goods depot had closed in June 1964, the old Midland Railway warehouse survived and was still standing 12 years later, as can be seen behind the train. *(Clive Weston)*

The low early afternoon sun casts autumn shadows over the site of Apperley Bridge goods yard as 47588 passes with the 1040 from Carlisle to Leeds on 22 November 1983. As we saw in the previous photograph, taken in 1976, the goods shed survived track lifting and the demolition of other smaller buildings in the yard area but the site was earmarked for a housing development and it had gone by the time of this view. This Class 47 was new in 1964 as D1773 and had four identities and two names during its 39-year career. It became 47178 in the TOPS system in 1974, then 47588 in June 1983. In July 1988, while part of the Railfreight Distribution pool, it was named *Carlisle Currock* then, having been transferred into the Rail Express Systems pool, it was re-named *Resurgent* in 1992. Its final identity was 47737 which it carried from 1995 until withdrawal in 2004. *(Alan Whitaker)*

The branch to Ilkley from Apperley Junction was double track throughout until March 1983 when it was singled to Esholt Junction, then on into Guiseley station. The Shipley line from Guiseley Junction was also singled at the same time. These changes prompted closure of Esholt Junction signal box. Double line operation then resumed between Guiseley and Ilkley. A two-car Class 108 DMU, in BR's revised off-white and blue livery, climbs from Apperley Junction to join the branch from Shipley and Baildon at Esholt Junction on an evening service from Leeds to Ilkley in May 1976. Although preferable to the boring all-over blue applied to the DMU fleet from 1967, the predominantly off-white colour scheme was difficult to keep clean so it was replaced by an alternative blue and grey livery which was adopted as standard from the late 1970s. *(Clive Weston)*

A Metropolitan-Cammell Class 101 DMU calls at Guiseley station with a Leeds-Ilkley service on 24 July 1973. Unusually for the time, it is displaying the correct B3 headcode. These headcodes were dying out by then and were removed on refurbishment of DMU stock later in the 1970s. However, the destination display says 'Leeds City' which is where the train has come from, not where it is going. Well, you can't have everything! The impressive Midland Railway footbridge linking the platforms was removed on 3 May 1992, prior to electrification work, and was taken to Kirkby Stephen station on the Settle & Carlisle line where it was re-erected and continues in service today. Guiseley station became unstaffed for passengers in October 1968 but was still manned for parcels traffic for a while longer. The main station building was demolished after the parcels business ceased. The platform gas lights were fitted with timers after the station staff were deployed elsewhere as there was nobody to switch them on manually. *(Stuart Baker)*

Sunday engineering diversions during June 1975 brought the rare sight of locomotive-hauled passenger trains on the Ilkley line. The afternoon London St. Pancras to Glasgow, seen here during an engine change at Guiseley station on 15 June, had been diverted from the main line at Apperley Junction and continued to Guiseley where it had to reverse. The locomotive which had worked the train from Leeds was detached and another attached at the other end. The train then ran to Shipley Guiseley Junction to re-join the main line and continue its journey north. Nearest to the camera is 45016 which would work the train to Glasgow. Under the footbridge in the distance is 45109 which had been detached, having brought the train from Leeds. The signal box survived until electrification of the line in 1994 and was then moved to the Embsay & Bolton Abbey Steam Railway. The goods shed on the left also survived and is now occupied by a firm of building materials suppliers. The two diesels fared less well and were scrapped in the same Leicester yard within weeks of each other at the end of 1986, with both having completed 25 years in service. *(Willowherb Publishing Archive)*

A major programme of track relaying and other works in the Ilkley area in the winter of 1978 brought weekend engineering trains to the line. Bradford Valley goods yard was used as the hub for the operations and numerous locomotives and permanent way wagons associated with the works could be found gathered there on Saturday nights in preparation for their Sunday duties. On 22 January 1978, one of the engineers' workings is seen accelerating through Guiseley station from the Ilkley direction, double-headed by two Class 40s. The leading loco is 40192 which has had its four-character headcode equipment replaced by marker lights. BR began to dispense with the requirement for train reporting headcode displays on main line diesels from 1975. *(Alan Whitaker Collection)*

Local goods traffic on the Wharfedale line saw a slow decline through the 1960s and, by the time of this view on 14 April 1973, only Guiseley and Menston were still open as coal concentration depots. The morning trip from Bradford Valley is seen here being shunted in Menston yard by Sheffield Tinsley's Class 25 No. 5228 which had been borrowed by Leeds Holbeck to work the train. Until January 1975, the return working had to go to Ilkley to run round but this was inefficient and time-consuming. New arrangements were then put in place to permit the locomotive to propel the brake van and empties wrong line between Menston and Guiseley where it was able to run round and regain the line to Baildon and Bradford. Coal deliveries to Guiseley ceased in January 1981 but Menston continued to be served until June 1982. Further up the line, Burley-in-Wharfedale had closed to goods in 1964, with Ben Rhydding following in 1965 and Ilkley in 1967. *(Stuart Baker)*

A Class 108 DMU, comprising power car No. 50612 (leading) and driving trailer car No. 56205, pulls into Burley-in-Wharfedale station on an Ilkley to Bradford service in March 1976. Both cars in this view had been part of the Bradford Manningham allocation in the early 1960s, although not paired together at that time. The Class 108s working the Wharfedale and Airedale lines retained a First Class section until 1983 when they became Standard Class throughout. This set is sporting the revised off-white and blue stripe DMU livery, first introduced in 1975. Such a predominantly light colour scheme proved impractical in terms of cleanliness and was already being phased out by 1980. Burley-in-Wharfedale station had been reduced to an unmanned halt in October 1968 and demolition of the platform buildings took place between April and June 1973. They were replaced by small stone-built waiting shelters in August 1973. The platforms were raised and resurfaced in 1975 when electric lighting replaced the gap lamps. A lone passenger can be seen emerging from one of the new shelters as the train arrives. *(Martin Bairstow)*

Another Class 108, this time in the earlier all over blue DMU colour scheme, calls at Ben Rhydding, its last intermediate stop between Leeds and Ilkley, on 23 February 1974. The First Class section of the train is marked by the yellow line over the first two windows. As at neighbouring Burley-in-Wharfedale, the station had been unstaffed since 1968 and had undergone major changes in 1973 with small stone waiting shelters replacing its more substantial original buildings. The gas lighting column near the bottom of the footbridge staircase on the right was replaced by electric equipment in 1975 when the platform levels were raised. The bridge itself was removed as part of the 1990s Wharfedale line electrification programme. *(Martin Bairstow)*

A quiet interlude at Ilkley station in 1978 finds four Metro-Cammell DMUs awaiting their next duties. The unit on the right is stabled on the rusted track alongside Platform 4 which had been the Up 'through' platform from Skipton until the line was axed in 1965. Although it continued to be used to stable empty units, this platform was closed to passengers but it was not officially abandoned until September 1983 when the station was reduced to two platforms. *(Jan Rapacz Collection)*

Photographer Stuart Baker stopped by to capture the familiar face of a Class 108 DMU in this evocative view at Ilkley station on 1 April 1974. The unit, with DMBS (Driver Motor Brake Second) car No. 50601 facing the camera, had just arrived from Leeds. Much of the attractive 1950s tangerine-coloured North Eastern Region enamel signage was still in place at a time when new corporate white and black metal signs were replacing the distinctive regional colours at stations all over the country. The original 19th century wrought iron platform canopies also add a sense of timelessness to the scene. The 'middle line' between Platform 1, on which the photographer is standing, and Platform 2, which is occupied by the DMU, was a former carriage siding. It was disconnected in March 1976 and later lifted. These platforms became the only two in operation after Platforms 3 and 4 were abandoned in 1983. They were shortened by 50 yards in 1986. Following closure of the Skipton line, there had been plans to demolish Ilkley station and re-site it further to the east but these were not progressed. Instead, part of the station was sold for commercial use and a new passenger entrance was created. *(Stuart Baker)*

Following closure of the Skipton line to all traffic in January 1966, a buffer stop was quickly erected at the end of Platform 3 which was still used by passengers. The other 'through' line which ran alongside Platform 4 was retained for track-lifting trains. These started running in April 1966 and the job was completed in June. Then, in July 1966, the landmark Brook Street bridge was demolished and another buffer stop was installed at the Skipton end of Platform 4. Fortunately, BR did not bother to seal up the gap at the end of the platforms, thereby enabling this photograph to be taken from the short remnant of track formation still left between the station and Brook Street. The DMU standing at Platform 3 in this 1975 view is a Class 105 Cravens set which was working from Leeds Neville Hill depot at the time. These attractive and comfortable units - built between 1956-59 - were never synonymous with the Ilkley line but became more frequent visitors in the late 1970s/early 80s. *(Alan Whitaker Collection)*

A sign of things to come at Ilkley on 4 June 1981 as the unique Class 140 prototype 'Pacer' unit pauses in Platform 3 after a trial run from Leeds. 140001 was built at Derby in 1980 using adapted Leyland Bus components. The cabs were a separate design as, understandably, BR wanted something more robust than a bus front. Withdrawals of some of the 1950s first generation DMU types had begun in the late 1960s, while others were selected for refurbishment to prolong their lives. But the BR hierarchy knew that refurbishment would only buy time and that a comprehensive programme of replacement would soon be needed. The 'Pacer' railbus concept was the first step in that programme. 140001 was tested on various parts of the network and was successful enough to prompt orders for improved versions which would become Classes 141-144. The prototype was short-lived in public service and became a Departmental unit before being sold into preservation in 1995. Ilkley's tall Midland Railway signal box can be seen just beyond the bridge. It was erected in 1913 and remained in operation until 12 June 1994 when electronic signalling was introduced as part of the electrification programme. It was demolished a week later, on 19 June. *(Robert Anderson)*

The unusual sight of a locomotive-hauled passenger train at Ilkley station on the evening of 28 July 1985 as 'Peak' No. 45123 The *Lancashire Fusilier* stands in Platform 1 after arrival with a *T.P. Tours* charter. The train had left Ilkley that morning behind Class 47 No. 47052 which worked it as far as Leeds. 45123 then took over for the run to Carlisle via Newcastle and the Tyne Valley line, which included a brief stop at Hexham. The tour then returned from Carlisle via Settle. This 'Peak' was the fifth of 25 in the class to be named after British Army Regiments. The naming ceremony, conducted by Brigadier P.G. Bamford CBE DSO, took place at Manchester Piccadilly station on 31 October 1963. 45123 was new in June 1962 as D52. With front end train reporting headcode panels no longer required, it was fitted with sealed marker lights in 1978. The locomotive continued in service until July 1987. After yielding spares to keep other 'Peaks' in operation, it was cut up in 1988. *(Alan Whitaker)*

A rare DMU at a rare event. The weather wasn't kind but 5 January 1973 was a day of celebration in Baildon. Reopening of stations at this time was very unusual but Baildon had a big advantage. Although the main station building had been sold following closure in 1953, the platforms had never been removed so could be brought back into service quite cheaply. And when Baildon Urban District Council offered to cover the cost of restoration it was a 'no brainer.' In spite of the wet weather, a sizeable crowd turned out to welcome the reopening day 'Special' and to witness Baildon UDC chairman, Arnold Lightowler, doing the honours. The special train was a Class 109 Wickham unit, comprising cars E50416 and E56171. This was one of only five such sets ordered by BR. They entered service in 1957 but two were later sold back to the manufacturer and exported to Trinidad. The last active set was withdrawn in 1971. The unit seen here had been withdrawn in 1967 and was subsequently converted into the Eastern Region General Manager's saloon, complete with its own kitchen. It continued in that role until 1980 and was then sold into preservation – the only one of its type to survive. *(Clive Weston)*

A diverted Glasgow Central to London St. Pancras climbs through Baildon station behind long-serving Leeds Holbeck 'Peak' No. 45013 (formerly D20) on Sunday, 15 June 1975. Judging by the exhaust being thrown out, the locomotive is working hard. 45013 would be detached from the train at Guiseley where classmate 45109 was waiting to take over for the run to Leeds. Another reversal and engine change would then be required before the nine-coach train could continue its journey south. Baildon was still a double track station at this time, with both platforms in use. Singling of the line from Guiseley Junction to Guiseley station in 1983 resulted in the Up platform (on the left) being abandoned. All services were then concentrated on the Down side where the main station entrance is located. 45013 was one of 70 Peaks built with 'split-box' headcode equipment. These boxes were removed from some locos in the late 1960s and replaced by a central panel but most retained their original look until headcode displays became obsolete and sealed marker lights were fitted. 45013 remained in service until 1987 and was scrapped a few years later. *(Willowherb Publishing Archive)*

Patronage at Baildon was steady, if unspectacular, until electric trains were introduced on Bradford to Ilkley services in 1995. This prompted a gradual increase, particularly in morning and evening commuter business and before the interruptions caused by the Covid-19 pandemic in 2020/1, the station was being used for more than 100,000 journeys a year. This view dates from 16 July 1977 and shows passengers disembarking from a Class 101 DMU on an afternoon Bradford Forster Square to Ilkley service. *(Martin Bairstow)*

A classic view of the Shipley Curve on a bright 16 November 1974 before the construction of platforms was even thought about. After easing off the power on the approach to Leeds Junction, the driver of 'Peak' No. 58 *The King's Own Royal Border Regiment* cranks it up, releasing a burst of exhaust. The train is 1S68 – the erstwhile *Thames-Clyde Express* for Glasgow Central. Until its closure in 1966, Glasgow St. Enoch's station had been the destination for this service. D58, as it was when built in 1962, was named at Carlisle Citadel station on 1 May 1963. It became part of the Leeds Holbeck allocation in 1972 and stayed for five years before its transfer to Sheffield Tinsley. The locomotive received its 45043 TOPS number in February 1975 and continued in service until 1984. Leeds Junction signal box, which can be seen to the right of the trailing coaches, closed in July 1975. *(John S. Whiteley)*

Another view of 1S68 as it accelerates off the Shipley Curve at Bingley Junction behind 'Peak' No. 45036 on Sunday, 22 June 1975. The locomotive is crossing the connection to the Angle Sidings, referred to on Page 37. These still saw occasional use but the connection was severed in September 1978, eight months before a platform was built on the Down side of the Shipley Curve. The rock face on the left was a familiar landmark which had provided a precarious vantage point for some members of the local train spotting fraternity in the days of steam when the line was much busier. This 'Peak' began life as D45 in September 1961 and was a regular performer on the Glasgow services through Shipley between 1972 and 1977 when it was based at Leeds Holbeck. It was withdrawn in 1986. *(Willowherb Publishing Archive)*

Two years after stripping the long established *Thames-Clyde Express* of its title, BR axed the service completely from May 1976. It was replaced by two separate trains. The first ran from London St. Pancras to Nottingham where it terminated. The other started at Nottingham and ran to Glasgow Central via Leeds and Carlisle. The formation initially comprised nine coaches and a buffet car, the same as had been used for the *Thames-Clyde Express*, but this began to vary and buffet provision was sometimes missing. The Nottingham services lasted until May 1982 when they were reduced to Leeds-Carlisle only. On a snowy 13 February 1978, Healey Mills Class 40 No. 40148 rounds the Shipley Curve with the morning Nottingham-Glasgow which it had taken over at Leeds. The headcode display is set at four zeros which was an interim arrangement until locomotives were fitted with marker lights. *(John S. Whiteley)*

BR's behind the scenes scheming to create a spurious case to close the Settle to Carlisle line was in full swing in the early 1980s. The withdrawal of the Nottingham-Glasgow trains from the start of the new timetable in May 1982 - and their replacement by Leeds-Carlisle services running at inconvenient times - was part of a 'closure by stealth' process. Happily, the BR case was discredited by a well organised protest campaign and the line was saved in 1989. It has since gone from strength to strength. This view of Class 47 No. 47443 arriving in the bi-directional Platform 5 at Shipley station with the 1040 Carlisle to Leeds dates from 2 July 1983 when the future of Settle line seemed bleak. This platform opened for Down trains only in May 1979 which meant that stopping trains from Skipton to Leeds still had to use the Bradford platform before reversing at Shipley Bradford Junction. A crossover to permit Up trains to run 'wrong line' into the new platform was installed the following year. The formation of the erstwhile Angle Sidings connection is evident between the signal box and the platform end. *(Alan Whitaker)*

It is now 11 June 1989 and 47443 is back at Shipley, having acquired a name and BR large logo blue livery with yellow cabsides. It is working the Sundays-only 1446 Leeds to Carlisle service which was loaded to only four coaches. The locomotive was named *'North Eastern'* in May 1988 and continued to be a regular performer on the Leeds-Carlisle return workings until April 1990 when Class 31s started to appear more frequently on these trains. It began life in 1964 as D1559 and was renumbered into the TOPS system as 47443 ten years later. It survived in service until 1993 and was cut up at Crewe Works in 1996. *(Alan Whitaker)*

The iconic Salts Mill provides a magnificent backdrop for this Class 47, heading a seven-coach Nottingham train between Saltaire and Shipley on Friday, 24 March 1978. It appears that no buffet car was provided on this day. The train was non-stop between Keighley and Leeds as the platform on the Shipley station avoiding curve, and the crossover to access it from the Up line, were still some way off. Salts Mill was built between 1851 and 1853 at the behest of its founder, the eminent and ground-breaking industrialist, Sir Titus Salt. As well as the mill, he commissioned a 'model village' of housing for his workers and a church. Saltaire is now a UNESCO World Heritage Site. *(John S. Whiteley)*

A few years earlier, in the summer of 1974, the London St. Pancras to Glasgow Central climbs towards Saltaire behind 45006 *Honourable Artillery Company* - one of the first named 'Peaks' allocated to Leeds Holbeck. It arrived in August 1968 as D89, along with D53 *Royal Tank Regiment* and D60 *Lytham St. Annes*. The trio were regularly rostered for express passenger workings through the Aire Valley at the time. As well as the *Thames-Clyde Express*, there was the morning Leeds to Glasgow express (Sundays excepted) and *The Waverley* from London St. Pancras to Edinburgh which ran north of Carlisle via Hawick on the Waverley Route until its closure in January 1969. 45006 remained a Holbeck loco for ten years until 1978. It was in traffic until 1986 when its 25½ years of service was brought to a conclusion. It was scrapped in 1988. *(Willowherb Publishing Archive)*

Perhaps nowhere was the folly of the closure and demolition of all the intermediate stations between Bradford, Leeds and Skipton better illustrated than at Saltaire. Less than 20 years after the deed was done, the world famous heritage village had its station restored on the same site. This is the location a year before reopening when the new station scheme was in the final stages of the planning. Pairs of Class 31s on the 'Tilcons' were a familiar feature of railway operations in the Aire Valley between the late 1970s and 1991 when Class 37s briefly took over. These were only a stop-gap and were soon replaced by brand new 3,100 horsepower Class 60s. Here, 31322 and 31199 head a Rylstone (Swinden Quarry) to Hull past the site of the former Saltaire station platforms on 22 March 1983. *(Alan Whitaker)*

Saltaire's new station had to be carefully designed to blend in with the surrounding conservation area. Special features included Victorian-style lamps and stonework similar to that used to build the original 1856 station. Construction began in September 1983 and it opened to passengers on 9 April 1984. The cost was £135,000. A year later, the station won a prestigious design award in an annual competition sponsored by the famous transport publishing company, Ian Allan. To mark the reopening, a special return trip to Leeds was provided for guests on a new Class 141 'Pacer' unit. This view shows the celebrity Class 40, No. 40122/D200, arriving at Saltaire on one of its regular jobs - the 1040 from Carlisle to Leeds - on 27 July 1985. *(John S. Whiteley)*

The Government's rejection of BR's bid to close the Settle-Carlisle line prompted a positive initiative by Regional Railways North East to boost 'off season' revenue. This unexpected marketing ploy involved running some of the Saturday Leeds-Carlisle services with locomotive types that would not normally work such trains. The initiative paid off handsomely with passenger numbers swelled by enthusiasts keen to sample the rare motive power. The idea was to team up the normal rostered Class 47 (needed to provide train heating) with freight locomotives. These trains operated on all four Saturdays in November 1989 and the response was so spectacular that they ran again on five more Saturdays in February and March 1990. This is the 1045 Leeds to Carlisle on 10 March 1990, being triple-headed through Saltaire by a pair of Hunslet-Barclay Class 20s, Nos. 20905 *Iona* (leading) and 20906 *Georgina*, and 47422. The ensemble had passed through earlier on the 0634 ex-Carlisle. The 20s had been sold by BR to Hunslet-Barclay for contract freight use so to see them back on a scheduled main line passenger train was certainly worth a photograph, even in less than ideal weather conditions. *(Alan Whitaker)*

A beautifully composed view of Sheffield Tinsley's 'Peak' No. 45038 as it powers the morning Nottingham-Glasgow away from Saltaire on 5 April 1978. This vantage point from Hirst Lane bridge enabled the photographer to embrace a number of local landmarks, including the Leeds-Liverpool Canal and Saltaire cricket ground to the left and, behind in the distance, the dome of Saltaire Congregational Church (now the United Reformed Church), a Grade 1 listed building dating from 1859. The 'Peak' was almost 17 years old at the time of this view, having emerged new from Derby Works as D48 in 1961. It still had another seven years of life ahead of it, being withdrawn in 1985. *(John S. Whiteley)*

Another view from the Hirst Lane bridge, this time looking north, finds Glasgow Eastfield's Class 47 No. 47541 *The Queen Mother* approaching with the 1040 Carlisle to Leeds on 20 June 1983. The naming of 47541 by the Queen Mother herself at Aberdeen station nine months earlier had been the first time since the days of steam that a member of the Royal Family had named a railway locomotive. It was not uncommon for locos based at Scottish depots to retain their snowploughs all year round, whether the temperature was minus zero or scorching, so the sight of 47541 with its ploughs in the heady heat of late June was no great surprise. Some Carlisle-Leeds diagrams were worked by Class 47s from depots as far afield as Inverness and Plymouth Laira in the 1983-87 period. It was impossible to predict what might turn up which made things interesting. 47541 started life as D1755 in 1964, allocated to Landore (Swansea). Having been renumbered again in 1994, it was withdrawn as 47773 in 2004 after almost 40 years' service and is now preserved. *(Alan Whitaker)*

On Saturday 17 March 1990, Class 56 heavy freight locomotive No. 56075 *West Yorkshire Enterprise* was paired with Class 47 No. 47453 for the 0825 Leeds to Carlisle. The popularity of these unusual combinations was such that the trains had to be strengthened to cope with demand. On this occasion, the trailing load is ten coaches rather than the usual four or five. The train is about to pass over the Hirst Wood foot crossing near the site of a private siding which served local engineering firm F. Wigglesworth & Co. for many years. The siding connection was controlled by Hirst Wood signal box, which stood on the Up side of the line towards Hirst Lane bridge. It was abolished in 1972. 56075 was built at Doncaster Works in 1980 and was named at Leeds City station on 9 July 1985. It remained in service until 2004 and was then cut up by Rotherham scrap dealers, C.F. Booth. 47453 (new as D1571 in 1964) was withdrawn in 1992 and held in store for five years before being scrapped. *(Alan Whitaker)*

Train loads of newly quarried ballast from Ribblehead to Healey Mills was a regular traffic flow on the Aire Valley line well into the 1980s. Here, Class 47 No. 47201 enters Hirst Wood cutting, having just crossed the River Aire bridge. These trains were worked by pretty much anything available, with Classes 25, 31, 40, 45 and 47 all taking their share of the duties. However, such a menial task was totally out of keeping with the early history of this particular Class 47. It emerged from Crewe Works in 1965 as D1851 and was one of a group of 47s mainly dedicated to express passenger and freight services on West Coast main line between Crewe and Glasgow before the arrival of the more powerful Class 50s in 1968/69. Their duties were more mixed after that but they still clocked up the miles on the WCML until electrification was completed in 1974. 47201 enjoyed a long career of almost 42 years. It was scrapped shortly after withdrawal in 2007. *(Alan Whitaker)*

Any appearance by a Class 40 during 1984 attracted attention as the number of active locomotives dwindled almost week by week. The evening Newcastle to Clitheroe cement tanks train occasionally turned up a '40' as was the case on Wednesday 4 July 1984 when 40155 was in charge. It is seen here crossing the River Aire just north of Hirst Wood. The loco would run round the train at Hellifield before taking the Ribble Valley line to the cement works at Clitheroe. 40155 lasted another six months and was still in working order when it was withdrawn as 'surplus to requirements' on 22 January 1985. After a long period in store at Crewe, it was cut up. *(Alan Whitaker)*

A regular Class 40 duty in 1984 was the Tuesdays-only Workington to Sheffield scrap train. The working was such a good bet to see a '40' in action that it attracted much interest from enthusiasts. That said, only the photographer was present to witness 40143 accelerating its long rake of loaded scrap wagons through Bingley station after a signal stop on 31 July 1984. By the middle of January 1985, it was all over and the 40s had been replaced on the 'scrapper' by Class 25s and 47s. 40155, seen on the previous page, was the last of the class to work a scrap train on the Airedale line when it appeared on a Friday working from Barrow to Sheffield on 18 January 1985 – four days before its withdrawal. 40143 - one of only 20 Class 40s fitted with split headcode boxes - was taken out of service on the same day as its classmate and was scrapped at Crewe in 1986. *(Alan Whitaker)*

40079 was another of the small band of Class 40s kept in service until early 1985 when all but the 'celebrity' D200/40122 were withdrawn. It is seen here about to depart from Bingley on 1M26 - the 1555 from Leeds to Carlisle - on 2 September 1984. It was the only Class 40 to have worked anywhere in West Yorkshire that day, according to one of the photographer's contacts in the BR Operating Department. Although not officially sanctioned, 40079 also carried its pre-TOPS number (279) in common with several other members of the class which ran with dual identities during their last year in service. Bingley station still reeks of its Midland Railway heritage, although it was clearly due a facelift after years of minimum maintenance. It had to wait another 13 years. In 1996/97, the station underwent major restoration with all its historic features retained. It has since been fitted with a passenger lift on each platform, carefully designed to protect the integrity of the station's heritage. *(Alan Whitaker)*

The village of Crossflatts, near Bingley, waited more than a century for its own station. Lobbying for a station to be built there began in 1875 but was rejected by the Midland Railway Company's Directors who felt it was too close to the original Bingley station. The clamour grew louder when the current Bingley station was opened in the town centre in 1892 as this was further away than its predecessor. But the MR would not be swayed and it was another 90 years before Crossflatts had a station to call its own. The new station opened on 17 May 1982 as part of a long term programme of network improvements ushered in by the West Yorkshire Passenger Transport Executive which had taken over responsibility for local public transport strategy and decision-making in 1974. After years of closures and decline under BR, it was a new dawn. Five days after opening, Crossflatts passengers wait to board a Leeds-bound Class 108 DMU. The basic wooden platform surfaces were soon found to be lethal in wet weather and were subsequently improved. *(Martin Bairstow)*

'Peak' No. 45070 is about to pass under the A650 Bradford Road bridge just before Crossflatts station with the 1150 Glasgow Central to Nottingham on 27 September 1980. This had been a four track section until May 1967, when the Up and Down Slow lines were abandoned. The buildings to the right of the train were swept away to make space for the new Bingley by-pass dual carriageway which opened in 2003. 45070 entered service as D122 in October 1961 and lasted until 1987. It was scrapped in 1989. *(John S. Whiteley)*

Another regular locomotive-hauled passenger service on the Airedale line in the mid-1980s was the Hull to Lancaster, usually operated by a Class 31/4. These trains later ran to Carlisle instead of Lancaster and started at York on Sundays, but they were cut back to start at Leeds every day from May 1987. Some scheduled loco-hauled summer services from Leeds to Morecambe were then introduced in 1988 and again between July and September 1989, after which they were replaced by DMUs. 31446 is seen here passing Keighley Gasworks on the afternoon Hull-Lancaster on 5 August 1985. The train is passing the site of Thwaites Junction signal box which, for many years, controlled access into private sidings serving the Gasworks. The box was abolished in July 1967 and the gas holder seen here on the left was demolished in 2022. *(Alan Whitaker)*

Dismantling of the Midland Railway platform canopies on BR's side of Keighley station began in the early 1970s when the glass roof panels were removed. By the time of this view on 17 March 1977, only the redundant wrought ironwork remained, but not for much longer. To add to the general air of decline, the station clocks are showing different times. The vintage clock on Platform 1 is showing 9.14 while the smaller timepiece on Platform 2 claims that it is 1230. Which of them, if any, was correct was not recorded as this Class 108 DMU arrives on a Skipton to Leeds service. The 'General Waiting Room' and 'Platform No. 1' signs were 19th century survivors from Midland Railway days. The original blue and white enamel plates were covered over by BR in the 1950s and were not replaced until new corporate signage was installed about a year after this photograph was taken. When the old MR boards were taken down, some of the original enamel could be seen poking through. *(Clive Weston)*

The old station clock, vintage signage and canopy ironwork had gone from Keighley's Platform 1 as 'Peak' Class 46 No. 46053 rolls in with the 1150 from Glasgow Central to Nottingham on Good Friday, 4 April 1980. The wooden end boards of the covered passenger access ramp were repainted as part of minor improvement works in 1978/9. 46053, which was in the last year of its operational life, appeared earlier on Page 46 before renumbering and with its original front end design. Some may argue that sheeting over the headcode panel to accommodate new marker lights improved the look but many 'Peaks' now in preservation have had their headcode equipment restored – and they look better for it. The 'Peaks' had a long association with the Airedale line which began in 1961/62 when they ousted steam on most of the principal long distance passenger workings. Twenty years later, their appearances were becoming less frequent and they had all but vanished on normal scheduled services by May 1986. They did, however, continue to be seen on special workings and charter trips until 1989. *(Alan Whitaker)*

In the early days of the Keighley & Worth Valley Railway Preservation Society, BR retained access to Platform 3 at Keighley station for stabling parcels vans and DMUs while KWVR trains used Platform 4 which terminated at a buffer stop. The arrangement lasted until 1976 when the KWVR lease was extended so they were able to operate from both platforms. This view was taken on a very wet 21 July 1973 when BR and the KWVR were still working side by side. Nearest to the camera in Platform 3 is a two-car Birmingham Railway Carriage and Wagon Company Class 104 DMU which is laying over before returning to Bradford Forster Square. Platform 4 is occupied by the KWVR's German-built railbus No. 79964 which has just arrived from Oxenhope. This vehicle only spent nine years in BR service between 1958 and 1967 but, at the time of writing, was still going strong after 55 years on the Worth Valley line. *(Stuart Baker)*

Veteran Class 31 No. 31444 was the star of the show on 17 August 1988 when it was named *Keighley and Worth Valley Railway* to mark the 20th anniversary of the first public passenger trains to run on the line in the preservation era. After the nameplates were unveiled in a ceremony at Keighley station, the '31' made two return trips to Oxenhope. It is seen back at Keighley after the first of those trips. 31444 was already almost 30 years ago at this time, having entered service as D5555 in 1959, so its day in the spotlight had been a long time in coming. In 1983, it had been saved from withdrawal after receiving a replacement cab donated by a less fortunate classmate, No. 31111 (seen earlier on Page 18). It soldiered on in service until 1995 and was scrapped. *(Alan Whitaker)*

Three years before the naming of 31444, the Keighley & Worth Valley Railway had hosted another naming event. The centre of attention that day - 8 August 1985 - was Class 47 No. 47421, seen passing through the partly demolished Ingrow West station on its way to Haworth where it would be named *The Brontes of Haworth*. It was another locomotive honoured with a name late in life, having been in service since 1963 when it emerged from the Brush Works at Loughborough as D1520. After the naming ceremony, 47421 went to Oxenhope, back to Keighley and then made another round trip before leaving the Worth Valley line and resuming its normal duties. With 25 years of relative anonymity now in the past, the Gateshead-based '47' enjoyed six years as a named locomotive before withdrawal in 1991. Ingrow West station was reborn in the late 1980s when the similarly designed disused station at Foulridge, on the former Skipton-Colne line, was dismantled stone by stone, then taken to Ingrow to be re-erected. *(Alan Whitaker)*

'Peak' No. 45074 heads the Nottingham-Glasgow out of Keighley on 14 June 1979. The former Midland Railway goods depot on the right was still open but traffic was light and all but essential sidings had already been lifted. From 1951, it had been known as Keighley North to distinguish it from the former Great Northern Railway depot across the road which was Keighley South. The distinction was not necessary after 1961 when the ex-GN yard closed but the 'North' identity remained for a few more years. The view from this vantage point today is in stark contrast to what was there in 1979. Instead of a goods yard and a scrap yard, the main line now passes between two supermarkets. After closure of Keighley goods in September 1982, the site was quickly redeveloped for Sainsbury's and preparatory building work began while track was still being lifted. The store opened in 1984. On the opposite side of the line, the scrap yard (on the site of the Keighley steam loco shed) has made way for an Asda store which opened in 2009. *(John S. Whiteley)*

A glorious summer's day at Utley finds Class 40 No. 40154 heading sedately towards Keighley with a rake of permanent way wagons bound for Healey Mills on 22 June 1981. The train included a motley rake of elderly wooden planked open wagons, long since withdrawn from normal service but maintained to main line standards for Departmental use. This was 40154's last summer in service. It was withdrawn in January 1982. *(Alan Whitaker)*

Steeton & Silsden was another victim of the 1965 closures but the more enlightened approach of the West Yorkshire PTE led to a new station being opened after a 25-year absence. It was built with staggered wooden platforms and welcomed its first passengers on 14 May 1990. Twelve days later, on Saturday, 26 May, Class 144 *'Pacer'* unit No. 144004 departs for Skipton with a service from Leeds. All 23 sets were built by BR using Alexander bus bodywork on a four-wheeled underframe. The first unit, 144001, emerged on 11 December 1986 for an official Press launch which included a trip from Leeds to Ilkley and Bradford Forster Square. The Class 144s were introduced as two-car units but the last ten were later strengthened with a centre car. They were sponsored from new by WYPTE and remained a familiar sight on the local network until 2020. Most are now preserved, including this example. The bridge spanning the station had opened in 1988 as part of a major road building scheme between Keighley and Cross Hills. The A6068 level crossing was then closed, along with the signal box that had controlled it. *(Alan Whitaker)*

The long reign of Class 31s on the Tilcon trains from Swinden Quarry on the Grassington branch came to an end during 1991 when they were briefly replaced by pairs of Class 37s. They, in turn, were ousted by Class 60s in 1992. One hundred of these 3,100 horsepower heavy haul freight locomotives were built by Brush Traction at Loughborough, the first of which entered service in 1990. This example is 60095 *Crib Goch*, then just two months old. It is seen approaching Cononley level crossing with the afternoon loaded Tilcons to Hull on 27 May 1992. Thereafter, Class 60s took over most of the heavy freight duties through Airedale and over the Settle & Carlisle line. Although just outside the West Yorkshire PTE area, Cononley is another intermediate station on the Skipton line to have reopened since the 1965 closures. This was a relatively cheap and straightforward project as the platforms had not been removed when the buildings were demolished in the 1970s. Because of that, the new station, which opened on 20 April 1988, cost £34,000 compared to the £270,000 that reportedly had to be spent to restore neighbouring Steeton & Silsden to the network. *(Alan Whitaker)*

Inter-City trains from Bradford to London were transferred from the Interchange station to Forster Square from 3 October 1988. The switch was regarded by BR as 'an experiment' and Bradford's last chance to retain Inter-City status. The 0711 to King's Cross, worked by an HST, was the first of these services. The line on Platform 2 was extended to facilitate longer trains as part of a £100,000 package of track, signalling and car parking improvements but the station still appeared downtrodden after years of decline. When East Coast Main Line Inter-City 225 electric trains began running to Leeds the following year, the complete sets were hauled by diesels for the last leg of their journey into Bradford. This arrangement continued until May 1992, by which time they were using the new Forster Square station, opened in June 1990. During construction of the new station, the line into Bradford was temporarily closed so the London trains terminated at Shipley. The empty stock was then dragged by a diesel loco to Skipton to run round before returning to Leeds. Class 31 No. 31461 is seen at the old station on one of the 'drags,' as these workings became known, on 26 May 1989. *(Peter Holden)*

By 1991, Class 47s had become the mainstay of the Leeds-Bradford 'drags.' The 1550 from London King's Cross to Bradford Forster Square is seen here passing the Crossley Evans scrap yard at Shipley behind Glasgow Eastfield's 47518 on 29 July 1991. Built in 1966 as D1101, the locomotive had only 15 more weeks left in service. It was withdrawn on 14 November and scrapped by M.C. Metals of Glasgow in 1994. At the time of writing, there had been no rail-borne traffic from the Crossley Evans site for several years but the siding connection has been retained for possible as future use. *(John S. Whiteley)*

The last Leeds to Bradford 'drag' emerges from Thackley Tunnel with 47500 in charge on 9 May 1992. HSTs then took over the London services until electric trains could run into Bradford under their own power in 1995. This '47' was one of four repainted in lined green livery in 1985 to celebrate the 150th anniversary of the Great Western Railway. They also received GWR-style cast number plates but, seven years on, the only evidence of this loco's more illustrious recent past was its faded green paintwork. As mentioned previously, this Thackley Tunnel bore had an older twin dating from 1846. The new tunnel was built alongside to double route capacity between Leeds and Shipley from two to four tracks. It opened in 1901 and, at 1,518 yards, is 22 yards longer than the its predecessor because of its slightly wider curvature. The 1846 bore closed in 1968 but it still throws up challenges. In 2016, a 61-metre section was filled in to safeguard the operational tunnel in which defects were developing due to ground movement. Another part of the disused tunnel had already been infilled for the same reason in 1986. *(Robert Anderson)*

The derelict remains of the old Forster Square station and Valley Road goods yard site overshadow the small new terminus which opened in 1990 – exactly 100 years after its predecessor which had itself replaced an earlier station dating from 1846. The environment around Forster Square was an eyesore for years with redevelopment of the vacant railway land slow to take place. The new Forster Square station welcomed its first passengers on 11 June 1990 but its official opening was delayed until 5 July 1993 when Regional Railways North East Director, Bob Urie, expressed his frustration at the lack of progress in developing the surrounding area. At first, access to the new station was via the old station entrance and along an abandoned platform but it was sealed off from Sunday, 3 November 1991 following a spate of muggings. Passengers were then directed to a new entrance. Demolition began on 18 March 1992 and, within a month, the site had been cleared. With electrification of the line into Bradford still four years away, a Class 142 'Pacer' sets out for Ilkley on 25 May 1991. *(D.J. Mitchell)*

Pressure by Bradford Council to ensure that East Coast Main Line electrification did not end at Leeds intensified during the late 1980s/early 90s and was supported by the city's *Telegraph & Argus* newspaper which printed thousands of 'Electrify Bradford' window stickers as part of its campaign to spread the message. Conditional approval for the Leeds North West Electrification Scheme, embracing the Airedale and Wharfedale lines and the branch from Shipley to Bradford Forster Square, was given by the Government in 1990 and, in 1992, it authorised the PTE to lease electric trains. The official launch by BR Chairman, Sir Bob Reid, took place at Leeds City station on 24 February 1992, although preparatory infrastructure work was already underway at several locations. With work quickly advancing, this was the scene looking towards Dowley Gap at Bingley on Sunday, 30 May 1993 where track was being lowered and realigned on the approach to the Leonard Street bridge and Bingley Tunnel. The loco in the distance is Class 31 No. 31247 which had shunted a rake of ballast wagons to where the men were working. *(Alan Whitaker)*

Keighley station was a building site on Sunday, 28 February 1993 as track and platform reconstruction works took place in preparation for electrification. This train of TOPE hopper wagons filled with spoil was headed by Class 47 No. 47522 *Doncaster Enterprise* in the early BR Parcels Sector livery of red and dark grey. This locomotive had previously carried an LNER-style apple green colour scheme applied in 1987 to coincide with its naming at Doncaster Works. It was new to York shed in November 1966 as D1105 and spent 32 years in service. Following privatisation of British Rail in 1994, it passed into the ownership of the freight operator English, Welsh & Scottish Railways and was withdrawn in December 1998. *(Alan Whitaker)*

Electrification engineering works in the Skipton area provided Railfreight Metals Sector Class 37 No. 37504 *British Steel Corby* with Sunday employment on 3 April 1994. These locos were not especially common on the Airedale line at the time so the appearance of this example heading through Crossflatts station with a mixed train of loaded spoil wagons and ballast empties was a welcome sight. 37504 emerged in 1962 as D6739 and, at the time of writing 60 years on, was still active as part of the Locomotive Services heritage fleet. It is now numbered 37603. A Keighley & District Travel Leyland Olympian double-decker, carrying the Northern Rose coach services branding of its predecessor, the West Yorkshire Road Car Company, crosses the railway on a service to Bradford. *(Alan Whitaker)*

A late autumn snowfall has created a wonderfully atmospheric scene at Shipley as night engineering work for electrification progresses on 21 November 1993. In charge of the works train is Class 31 No. 31547 in grey and yellow 'Dutch' livery which was adopted for locomotives in the civil engineers' pool in 1990. The livery style bore a striking resemblance to the corporate colours of Netherlands Railways, hence the nickname. The programme of preparatory works needed to lay the foundations for electrification of the Bradford, Ilkley and Skipton lines was complicated and immense and, from time to time, led to a requirement for line closures. For example, the Ilkley line was closed for six weeks in the summer of 1992 for major works which could never have been completed within the time limits of short weekend possessions. Similarly, the works at Keighley seen on Page 98 required a longer closure. By April 1994, wiring was appearing on some sections and the installation of new electronic signalling was progressing between Kirkstall, Ilkley and Saltaire. Masts to carry the overhead wires were also appearing in increasing numbers as momentum grew. *(Peter Holden)*

The impending privatisation of British Rail complicated efforts by West Yorkshire PTE to secure funding to lease new electric trains for the Bradford, Ilkley and Skipton services for which Government authorisation had been given in 1992. With completion of the scheme in sight and no prospect of any trains to run on the newly-electrified lines, BR offered a fleet of Class 308 units which were being displaced from Essex suburban services out of London. These units were almost 35 years old but the PTE was in no position to turn down the offer. The 21 sets destined for West Yorkshire were refurbished and repainted in 'Metro' red and cream livery. They were only ever intended as a stop-gap until new trains became available. The plan was to introduce electric trains between Leeds-Ilkley and Bradford in July 1994, with Skipton following in November, but these dates were put back and it was 25 May 1995 before 308138 became the first passenger carrying unit to work from Leeds to Ilkley. A few weeks later, sister unit 308136 is seen here slowing into Shipley on a Bradford-Ilkley service. *(Colour-Rail)*

308143 calls at Menston on an Ilkley-Leeds service soon after the introduction of electric trains on the route in 1995. The main station buildings at Menston were not demolished when the station was de-staffed in 1968 and survived intact for 30 years until ticket office staff were reintroduced in 1998. That was not the case at neighbouring Guiseley where a new ticket office building had to be constructed in 2002. Plans to install two stone-faced lift towers and modify the passenger footbridge to improve access for disabled people using Menston station were approved by Bradford Council in 2022. *(John Holroyd)*

An evocative late evening view of 308141 calling at Shipley on a service from Skipton to Leeds on 18 January 1997. Opening of the Up (Leeds) platform in 1992 required construction of a footbridge between the two platforms on the Shipley Curve, which can be seen over the train. Lifts alongside the bridge were added in 2009. At the same time, a new bridge with lifts was built to link the Leeds-Bradford and Bradford-Ilkley platforms to improve disabled access. Prior to that, it had only been possible to cross between these two platforms via a subway. Although only brought in as a stop-gap, the Class 308s operated for six years until new Spanish-built Class 333 units entered service in January 2001. By then, they were more than 40 years old and had become increasingly expensive to maintain. But, in spite of their age, the veteran sets still had fast acceleration and could provide a 'lively' ride. Rattling at speed through Thackley Tunnel could be quite disconcerting at times! Overall, they did their jobs well and attracted a cult following - even among railway staff. 308154 had the legend *'The Terminator'* inscribed above the guard's seat in the Motor Brake. *(Peter Holden)*

Three Class 321/9 electric units were built for West Yorkshire PTE in 1991 for use on Leeds-Doncaster services on which they stayed exclusively until the electric trains began running to Bradford, Ilkley and Skipton in 1995. Thereafter, they occasionally supplemented the 308s on morning and evening 'peak' services, although the Doncaster workings remained their main duties. The WYPTE trio (numbered 321901 to 903) were tagged on to BR's main order for 114 four-car Class 321 sets with 321903 the last off the production line. It is seen here at Bradford Forster Square awaiting departure for Leeds on 30 June 1996. All three 321/9s continued to operate from Leeds Neville Hill depot until 2020 when they were displaced by Class 331s. Five almost identical Class 322 trains brought in from Scotland in 2011 to bolster the local fleet were also displaced at the same time and all eight units then found work with Greater Anglia. *(Peter Holden)*

A large office block on the site of the old Forster Square station provides the backdrop to the replacement terminus in early 2001 as a Class 156 'Super Sprinter' No. 156468, in Arriva livery, prepares to depart for Carlisle. Bradford lost its direct services to the Border City in 1966 and, although it was good to see, this train did not signal the start of a revival. Leeds-Carlisle trains had been diverted to start and terminate at Forster Square because of engineering work between Kirkstall and Shipley. A fleet of 114 Class 156s were built between 1987-89 and took over most Regional Railways locomotive-hauled workings, including those on the Leeds-Settle-Carlisle line which were replaced on 1 October 1990. This photograph was taken from Ilkley-bound Class 308 electric unit No. 308158, for which the end was in sight as new Class 333s were already replacing the elderly 308s on Airedale and Wharfedale services. The old and the new worked alongside each other for a few months until all 16 Class 333 sets had settled into service. The 308s were then withdrawn. *(Alex Whitaker)*

The unique Class 89 No. 89001 and an unidentified Class 90 provide an unusual combination at the head of a London King's Cross train at Bradford Forster Square on 18 July 2000. 89001 was a prototype electric locomotive designed by Brush Traction and built in 1986 at BR's Crewe Works. Although it was a capable machine, no further orders were placed, with BR opting instead for a fleet of Class 91s to operate fast Inter-City services on its newly electrified East Coast Main Line. The '89' remained in service until 1992 and was then put into store. In 1996, it was bought and refurbished by Great North Eastern Railway which had just won the ECML franchise. It was withdrawn again after suffering a serious defect not long after this photograph was taken and, after a further period in store, was saved for preservation. At the time of writing, there were hopes that it would return to the main line as part of a heritage fleet, having undergone a long period of expensive restoration. The Class 90 was on hire to GNER as part of a long term arrangement to increase locomotive availability on the ECML. *(Peter Holden)*

In 1996, Great North Eastern Railway took over the East Coast Main Line franchise which came with a fleet of Inter-City 225 Class 91 locomotives, coaching stock and Driver Van Trailers (DVTs). After a successful first nine years, the franchise was renewed by the Strategic Rail Authority in 2005 but new financial complexities and the impact of competition on the East Coast route meant that GNER was unable to fulfil its commitments and it was replaced by National Express East Coast in 2007. Here, 91009 *The Samaritans*, resplendent in its GNER colours, passes Frizinghall on a Bradford Forster Square to London King's Cross train on 10 June 2000. After 30 years as the premier motive power on the ECML, the '91s' were replaced on many services by Hitachi-built 'Azuma' trains in 2019/20 and those that remained were then on borrowed time. *(Peter Holden)*

Apperley Bridge was another of the ten intermediate stations between Skipton, Bradford and Leeds wiped from the map in 1965 but now restored to the network, albeit on a different site. The new station, which has staggered platforms on either side of accommodation bridge No. 37, opened on 13 December 2015 and quickly proved popular for commuters weary of road congestion. Although platform facilities are basic, the station has a large car park which attracts 'park and ride' customers from a wide catchment area. This view dates from 14 July 2017 and shows numerous passengers disembarking from an evening 'peak' service from Leeds to Bradford Forster Square. A roadway for maintenance vehicles can be seen next to the platform. This uses the formation of the old Fast line and runs from Calverley to Thackley Tunnel. Apperley Bridge was the first station between Leeds and Shipley to reopen. It was followed in 2016 by Kirkstall Forge, designed to kick-start a large mixed development of housing and commercial properties and built some distance from the earlier Kirkstall station site. *(Martin Bairstow)*

A Class 142 'Pacer' diesel unit under the wires at Dowley Gap between Bingley and Hirst Wood on 12 July 1999. These trains were much maligned as they were often rostered for services for which they were never designed and which, therefore, seriously exposed their inadequacies. Travelling all the way from Leeds to Carlisle or Leeds to Morecambe on a 'Pacer' was very unwelcome for most passengers but it was not an uncommon practice. A total of 96 two-car Class 142 sets were built by Leyland Bus and British Rail Engineering Limited between 1985-87 and they gave 35 years of cheap and largely reliable service until the last examples were withdrawn in 2020. The unit seen here is 142069 which has just crossed the new Dowley Gap bridge over excavations which would become part of the Bingley by-pass road. It is carrying the attractive, but relatively short-lived, Regional Railways livery – a colour scheme which particularly suited these trains. *(Peter Holden)*

Locomotive haulage on Leeds-Settle-Carlisle services ended on Sunday, 30 September 1990, with Class 156 Super Sprinters taking over the following day. But, 13 years later, Arriva Trains Northern signed a contract with freight operator EWS to lease some of its Class 37/4s to 'top and tail' an extra daily semi-fast Leeds-Carlisle return service using four Mk. 2 coaches. This was a far more attractive proposition than the usual two-car Class 156 'stopper' and the Class 37-hauled trains proved very popular. After their return trip to Carlisle, the '37s' were also used to work a weekday evening 'peak' service from Leeds to Knaresborough and back and they proved popular on that line too. The leasing arrangement ended in 2004 when the Regional Railways North East franchise was transferred from Arriva to Northern Trains. Class 158 DMUs then took over and remain the usual motive power for Leeds-Carlisle services in 2022, even though they are now more than 30 years old. Back in the summer of 2004, when the 37s were still a familiar sight, snowplough-fitted 37405 is seen here at Keighley waiting to depart for Carlisle. *(Alex Whitaker)*

Loaded gypsum trains bound for British Gypsum's plaster and plasterboard works at Kirkby Thore, just north of Appleby, have been a staple of rail freight through the Aire Valley for many years. EWS Class 66 No. 66093 waits at a signal stop in Platform 1 at Shipley station on 1 August 2001 with empties for Drax. British Gypsum now has a contract to receive imported gypsum via Tees Dock and, at the time of writing, EWS Class 66s were still operating this traffic, although Class 60s appear occasionally. *(Martin Bairstow)*

The latest electric multiple units on the Airedale and Wharfedale lines are the Spanish-built CAF Class 331s, introduced in 2019 to replace the Leeds-based Class 321s and 322s. A total of 12 four-car sets are allocated to Leeds Neville Hill and work alongside the depot's Class 333s which have been familiar on Leeds-Ilkley/Bradford Forster Square and Skipton local services for more than 20 years. 331 110, which carries the name *Proud to be Northern*, is seen here at Ilkley after arrival from Leeds on 30 September 2019. The car park on the right covers the site of Platforms 3 and 4 which served the long lost 'through' line to Bolton Abbey and Skipton. The first Class 331s to be tested in the area were three-car sets. Thirty-one of these were built to work the electrified lines centred on Manchester and Liverpool but it was always intended that Leeds would receive higher capacity four-car units for its Ilkley, Skipton, Bradford Forster Square and Doncaster local services. *(Martin Bairstow)*